THE BIG BOX

ENGLAND'S ERA OF STEAM HAULAGE

T. McTaggart

DEDICATED TO THE LATE

W. MICHAEL SALMON M.R.C.V.S.

and

TOM B. PAISLEY M.A.

COVER PHOTOGRAPH

VM 2110 Atlas Fowler road locomotive. Ex. Norman E. Box now owned by Dr. J.D. Coombes, Firdale, 85 West Hill, Aspley Guise, Milton Keynes, England.

THE BIG BOX

T. McTaggart

Alloway Publishing

AYR

© T. McTaggart, 1986.

First Published in 1986
Reprinted in 1987
by Alloway Publishing Ltd.,
24 Beresford Terrace,
Ayr.

Printed in Scotland
by Walker & Connell Ltd.,
Hastings Square, Darvel,
Ayrshire.

ISBN 0 907526 27 6

ACKNOWLEDGEMENTS

The writing of this history was achieved only by the combined effort of many members of the Road Locomotive Society most of whom are named below:

The late Michael Salmon who started collecting historical information, the photographic collection of the late T.B. Paisley, John Mayes, ex Fowler driver with Pickfords the main supplier of information on N.E. Box operations, Steven Mustill ex MRS/E. Box Scammell driver, E. Box operations, Alan Duke, steam vehicle numbers, Les Burberry, archives photographs, Alan Martin general information, Mark Morgan, Researches in Liverpool, Iwan Jones, Welsh information, C.G. Mileham, Ferro-Concrete Bridge information, D. Marder for introductions also George Lea, A. Lamberton, W. Briggs, R. West, C. Lloyd, P. Smart, D. Stoyel, J. Thomas and J. Coombes. Non-members and sources who assisted include, E. Box, history of the family, Arthur Calvert ex 'Ajax' driver N.E. Box Ltd., John Wykes, roller information, A. Lomas, industrial consultant, Gordon Howarth, Wiltshire Newspapers Ltd., Liverpool Reference Library, Manchester Central Library, The British Commercial Vehicle Museum, Leyland, Lanc., The National Traction Engine Trusts magazine "Steaming".

Royalties from the sale of this book will go to the R.L.S. funds to assist with the cost of reproducing and maintaining archive photographs etc.

PREFACE

It may interest readers to know how the Road Locomotive Society came to have in its possession so many fine pictures of Norman E. Box's engines and tackle. In the summer of 1974 the late Michael Salmon received a letter from the Isle of Man merely addressed to the "President, Road Locomotive Society, Llandrindod Wells, North Wales". As he had moved to Norwich some 5 years previously, it is all credit to the Post Office that the letter was duly sent on to him.

The letter, from Mr & Mrs Sefton, N.E. Box's eldest daughter, contained the offer of all her late father's magic lantern slides. This was very readily accepted, and arrangements were made for the 2 wooden boxes of 150 3½ in. square glass slides to be despatched. These were collected from Altricham, Ches., by George Lea and delivered to Thursford, Norfolk. Michael Salmon collected them a few days later.

A cursory examination revealed that the size of the slides was to be a major problem in showing them until it was remembered that Richard Jolly of Oxford had a suitable old-time magic lantern. Which he readily agreed to bring to London, to a Committee meeting in the autumn of 1974. The slides were then examined and it was immediately realised the Society had been given a unique collection for its archives.

The then President of the Society, the late Tom Paisley, agreed there and then to have the old slides copied onto modern 2 in. square ones, and at the same time have black and white photographic prints made. The latter were invaluable in enabling members to identify and date many of the subjects. No notes were received with the slides and after much research nearly all the slides have now been identified regarding engines, loads as well as dates and places, giving a wide spectrum of heavy haulage during the 25 year period from 1910 to 1935.

As a postscript, Mrs Sefton who was informed of the work being done by the Society wrote to Michael Salmon in March 1976 that she was "simply delighted that Father's slides are proving so helpful and are giving such delight to your members and . . . . giving much pleasure to hundreds of people who are interested."

ALAN MARTIN
February 1986.

THE BIG BOX

A SON OF THE STEAM AGE

Norman Box, the heavy haulage pioneer, was born into a family which lived and breathed steam traction; a family which before the turn of the century, not only operated, but had patented design improvements to the steam traction engine. His grandfather William Box was a brick manufacturer from Market Lavington in Wiltshire. William was a shrewd and foresighted man, very much a family trait, who realised the potential of steam traction for his business. The first machine he bought to deliver his bricks was a Burrell No. 496 of 1871.

Meeting and marrying a local lass, the couple produced an inventive family of four sons. The Burrell had a profound effect on the Box boys, William Junior inventing a jackshaft to drive a traction engine rather than the previously used gear train or chains. This jackshaft connected the driving wheel to an eccentric mounted forward, producing a motion similar to that on a railway locomotive. Five of these jack-shafts were later built by Fowel, the first being shown at the RASE show at Liverpool in 1877, and another two were built by Robey.

Edward the musician of the family became bandmaster of the local brass band, but being a Box, the fund-raising opportunities of the steam traction engine were not lost on him. In 1878 it was decided to run a days excursion to Stonehenge, 14 miles away, using the Little Express traction engine. History relates that a fine day was had by all on this journey into the unknown world by steam haulage, complete with brass band.

The second son Alfred sought his fortune abroad, but William Junior, followed in his father's footsteps, opening a brickworks at Uffingston in Berkshire. However this enterprise was short-lived, for soon afterwards William identified the opportunities offered by an expanding Liverpool which was short of bricks. Moving to Aintree with his brothers Edward and Herbert and his second cousin Sam Rumble, a traction engine driver he opened a new brickworks. Edward brought his wife and eldest son Norman. Following family tradition, before he left Uffingston, William purchased a new Fowell with the Box jackshaft and also a Robey jackshaft.

1. — **Burrell No. 496 at Stonehenge. Note the front steering and chaindrive. W. Box brick maker.**

1a. — Excursion notice

BRICKS AND TRACTION

William and his family settled into, Hall Lane House, in Aintree in 1884 and he and Edward both expanded their fleet of traction engines. Edward bought a single crank Burrell No. 1061, named 'Oregon' and a Robey-Box jackshaft named 'Lion'. William ordered a Fowell Box patent traction engine No. 30, and in 1886 another No. 41. Road Locomotive Licences were issued for all of these engines.

The family's flair for invention was again illustrated when in 1884 William took out a patent to improve the road grip of traction engines. This method involved using coils of old rope bound around the wheels.

In 1885 Edward moved into new premises in Brazenose Road Bootle as Edward Box and Co. It was at this time that he bought his first Fowler No. 3628 (or 9) a single with church valve and 7'-6" driving wheels. Later he purchased a 6 NHP McLaren single No. 217, then a Marshall T.E. Edward Box became the first heavy haulier in Lancashire to use traction engines for contracting and the delivery of bricks, building his own trailers to go with the engines.

William, meanwhile, remained in charge of the brickworks, Edward splitting his time between the brickworks and his own venture in Bootle. Herbert left to go back to Market Lavington just before his father was tragically killed in 1894, run over by his own traction engine. Edward's main work then became moving Lancashire and other types of boilers for a few boiler makers and machinery of all types and sizes to and from the docks.

SOUTH AFRICA

John Fowler and Company of Leeds advertised in the trade papers for a representative to travel to South Africa to demonstrate and sell traction engines. Who better for this missionary work than Norman E Box, Edward's son Norman, had of course, grown up beside traction engines, learning how to drive, steer and even repair them. Fowler accepted the young Norman and it was arranged that he should take with him one of his father's drivers Tom Gray. It would appear that the visit was successful, but unfortunately, I can find no confirmation of this. In 1906 Norman returned home with his driver.

FATHER AND SON

Hearing that his son was coming home, Edward moved premises to Manchester, 13 Arch, Hyde Road, Ardwick, changing the firms's name to Edward Box and Son, in preparation of his eldest son joining the firm. He ordered a B6 Fowler Compound No 10325 called 'Titan'. With two four wheeled bogies, he began moving and erecting Lancashire boilers into position for operating. However when Norman arrived he revealed an independent streak and wanted nothing to do with his father's firm. Instead acquiring a single Fowler named 'Viking', he set up on his own account. With two traction engine wagons he began hauling lime to a tannery at Warrington, driving the engine himself. Norman hauled lime for a year until his father again approached him to join the new firm. With only his second cousin Sam Rumble to help him as foreman, Edward was overstretched trying to run both his Liverpool and Manchester operations.

2. — Fowel Box patent purchased by W. Box senior at Market Lavington and was later run over by it and died. Business sold to Holloway Bros. 1894.

After much discussion father and son ironed out an agreement. "Titan" would be transferred to Norman's name, and he would operate the firm (that is, I believe, the Manchester side of the business) as Norman E Box and Co but would give up the lime haulage. Norman Box was always his own man. Moving into the premises at 13 Arch he went into operation. In 1909 a second engine was passed to Norman, an 8NHP McLaren No. 1053 named 'Magic', later to have the registration No. NC 2027, along with two new four wheeled trailers.

From these beginnings in Ardwick, Norman Box started the firm which was to make his name famous in the world of heavy haulage.

THE GROWING BOX

Norman E Box was the second of the two great heavy hauliers to appear in Great Britian, the other being Glasgow's Thomas Currie Kerr. These two contemporaries had a long association, beginning in Manchester, where T C Kerr was a Director of the Enfield Cable Co. who gave quite a bit of cable moving to Norman.

In the early years of the century Manchester and district had numerous boiler and engineering works springing up, firms that, were later to become household names across the world, Galloways was one of Box's early customers. They made Lancashire boilers up to 40 tons and engines to drive cotton mills. Other early customers were Hargreaves of Bolton, Yates and Thom and Dunkinfield, all boiler and engine makers. Before the big electrical manufacturers came into being, the movement of boilers and heavy engines was the bulk of the heavy haulier's business. Even before the First World War, Norman Box, was moving railway out of gauge loads for Cammel lairds of Sheffield, part of the Birkenhead shipbuilding firm.

Just before the Great War, Norman Box purchased two second-hand Fowlers. The Fowler No. 9279, an A4, was resold in 1911 and the B6 No. 10142 was sold to P and H Shaw of Doncaster in 1919. He also had a new Fowler No. 13036, an R3 named 'Despatch' on Boulton wheels. These were hard wood packed rims on the driving wheels which raised the weight from approximately 12cwt to over a ton, and giving much better traction. Norman constructed his own wooden packed wheels instead of buying the patented variety. The next new engine arrived in October 1916 a B6 Fowler No. 14844, named 'Vulcan' later numbered NC 2022.

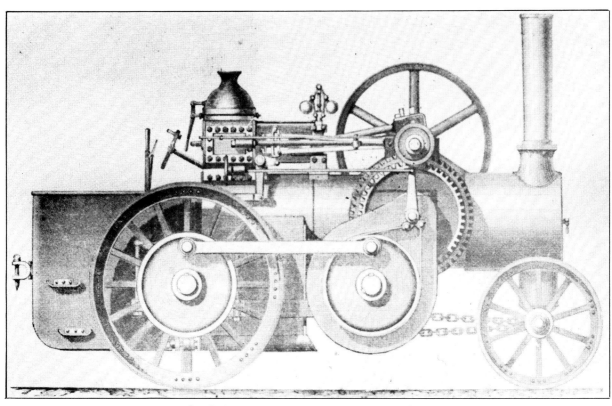

3. — Robey No. 5412 W. Box junior Uffington 1879.

4. — Fowell No. 2 W. Box junior Uffington 1877.

5. — Burrell Oregon with improved chain drive, on springs and cylinder close to chimney. Fowell Box patent No. 30 with the back axle behind the fire box hauling a marine boiler. Note the policeman to help with traffic control. Liverpool E. Box 1886.

6. — E. Box Liverpool Fowler with church valve fitted with crane in McLaren system of fitting crane No. 3628 about 1900. S. Rumble on footplate.

7. — E. Box Fowler No. 7863 with Edward on right removing coastal guns from the mouth of the River Mersey, 1921.

The earlier trailers were short four wheelers with turning lock and single turning bolster to be used with Lancashire boilers and other long loads. If the load was too long to allow the rear trailer to couple onto the front trailer, the drawbar was tied up to the load. This gave a delayed action to the steering of the rear end but worked very well. As these trailers could not take extra heavy concentrated loads Norman had Galloways, build six wheeled bogie's similar to a piano shifting bogie. Two wheels at each end on non-turning axles and two larger wheels on a centre axle.

Coal carrying wagons and living vans were added to the fleet, to be used on distance work. It must be realised by the reader that there were no cafes to cater for the road users in those days. It was from pub to pub that the hauliers moved, where the crews could find a hot meal and some entertainment to pass the evening hours.

The solid iron wheeled trailers and bogies were used right into the 1940's as the modern drop frame trailers did not appear until late 1928 on an idea by Thomas Currie Kerr of William Kerr and Co. of Glasgow. He had the first heavy drop frame trailer built at P and W McLellan Ltd of Glasgow, the well-known "Loch Ness Monster" which could carry in excess of 100 tons. The only change in the design of the original bogie was that later models had solid wooden brake blocks on screws to work on the rear wheels. It must be realised that hauling steel wheeled bogies took much more power than the more modern trailers and that

when the engines stopped pulling in most cases, the trailer stopped too. The brakes were, therefore non-essential except when crossing the Pennines when every means of slowing the load was used. The Fowlers of those days only had a screw brake on one wheel which was seldom used on the road as it only slewed the engine around. Most engines then had a flywheel brake which was only used for winching. The reversing lever was the only one which was of any practical use.

THE DEATH OF EDWARD BOX

Although his son had taken over the Manchester side of operations, Edward continued as a heavy haulier around Liverpool. During the Great War, his Fowler worked for the Ministry of Defence (War Office) setting up guns for coastal defence near the mouth of the Mersey. About this time he purchased two Liberty lorries and operated a Ford Model T van and a Vulcan maroon car. He also contracted to move portable engines and compressors mounted on top of a locomotive type boiler on a trailer, around the docks for Messrs Harland and Wolff of Liverpool. This contract lasted nearly twenty five years, long after Edward had left this life.

In 1921 Edward was to buy his last two engines. These were both second-hand, Fowlers No. 7963, Reg No. EM1174 and 8NHP B4 and No. 9983 Reg. No. EM1175 a B5 also of 8NHP fitted with a crane. Edward Box died in May 1925.

8. — E. Box & Son Fowler Titan No. 10325 with triple expansion crankcase, 1907.

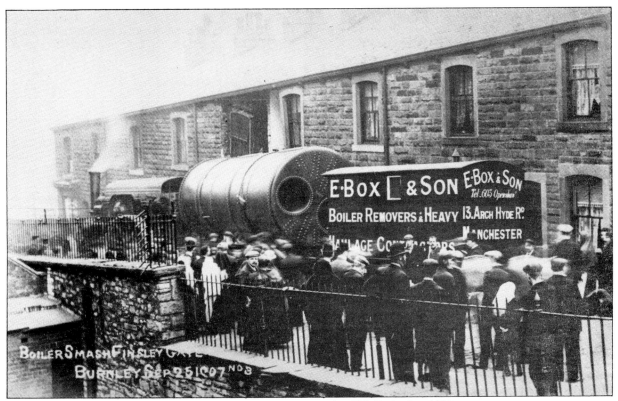

9. — E. Box & Son with Titan at Burnley 25th September, 1907.

10. — E. Box & Son with Titan another view of runaway, 1907.

On the death of his father, Norman's mother asked him to help to wind up her late husband's business. Considering Norman's determined independence from his father, it is perhaps not surprising that he refused the widow's request. Thus she was forced to turn to an ex-employee, Charles Gray, who was at that time in business for himself at Neston, to come across and value the business, In 1926 Gray himself bought the Fowler EM1174, the Marshall, and arranged for J. Routledge to buy the Fowler EM1175. The remainder of the engines were bought over by E. C. Marston of Marston Road Services Ltd. Norman had assumed that Marston would have been unable to buy over his father's business, but unbeknown to him Marston was financed by Hauliers Ltd. Although Norman had refused to become involved when his mother asked, he still felt justified in opening a family dispute over this rather sordid episode. It is ironic that while Norman took no concern of his father's affairs when he was alive, and even less when he was dead, he was furious that the business had been, as he claimed, undervalued.

OPERATIONS

All sorts of work was executed during the time of the Great War. One job involved supplying 32 ton loads of ballast to test two ferro-concrete bridges at, Ashton-Under-Lyne. One bridge for the Lancashire and Yorkshire Railway, being 180 feet long, and a 200 feet long bridge for the Great Central Railway. During that operation two traction engines, each hauling 32 tons, travelled side by side over two bridges. Given the 16 ton weight of the traction engines themselves this amounted to a total weight of 96 tons going over these bridges.

A job moved for the British Admiralty from the Midlands to Portsmouth required the road beneath a bridge to be lowered two feet to allow the load to proceed through Winchester. Norman notified the local authority telling them when the load would be travelling through. When the load arrived nothing had been done. However a phone call to the Admiralty brought out a squad of ratings complete with picks, shovels and barrows to move the offending two feet of road.

Restrictions like this happened all over the country and did not always end so peacefully. More often than not such restrictions resulted in a police summons for obstruction or for removing other such restrictions on the public highway. Occassionally Norman had a squad of navvies remove the road surface under a bridge then replace it when the load was through.

THE BOX GROWS

In and around the time of the Great War, Norman began to expand his fleet. Although some of his purchases were later resold, by 1917 he realised that the yard at 13 Arch was rapidly becoming too small for the growing fleet he now operated. A move was thus essential, and about this time, he transferred to his new premises at Rusholme Road, Ardwick Green, about half a mile away. The new office faced on to Maskill Street. In 1917 also, as a sympton of growth the company became Limited.

In 1913 Norman bought a new Burrell wagon, but sold it in 1914 to the Isle of Man. Strange to relate he began buying new tractors during the war. He bought his first, a Garrett No. 32680 Reg. No. BJ 2486 in 1915, which he kept until 1917, when he sold it to RF and FW Brown of Wallaton. In May of that year he bought another new Garrett No. 33032 Reg. No. BJ 3393, and in March he bought a new Burrell tractor No. 3752, selling it in 1919. Next he received a new Fowler tractor No. 14408 Reg. No. V4132 and two second-hand Fowler tractors, one a T1 from Mitchell of Bolton, BN925, but no maker's number: and No 11024 another T1 reg no. NC2028. The Fowlers did not last long and were resold in 1918, two going to Liverpool Corporation and the other to Sleaford. 1917 was a year of much toing and froing; in this year he also bought three second hand Garretts presumably to replace the tractors he sold in 1917. One of these tractors No. 32924 Reg. No. BJ3200 named "Briton" came from Briggs of Manchester, another No. 33646 Reg. TB 5143 came from Garstang RDC and the last No. 33410 Reg. No. BJ4549 came from R Dingle of Stokeclimsland. The latter was later resold to T. Cunlifte of Handsworth in Birmingham. He only purchased one Garrett with their famed super heater and it only lasted a short time before being resold no more were purchased only straight boilers being used.

In September 1918 a new Colonial tractor arrived, made by Aveling Porter, No. 8927, Reg. NC 2029, but was sold after a few years to Norman's father. Then in May 1919 a new Garrett No. 33503 Reg. BJ4312 named "Pilot" arrived. The next new Garrett was bought in February 1920 No. 33713 Reg. No. NC2024 and KJ4877 called "Trojan". This was the last of Norman's tractors, and it was sold later to HJ Pritchard of Peter Church.

As the First World War came to an end Norman bought a new McLaren 8NHP No. 1570 named "Rover", and in the same year he bought a second-hand Garrett 6 NHP No. 26695, Reg No. NC2026. Also in 1918, an Aveling and Porter single cylinder 8 NHP No. 3646 was bought for a special job and sold once the job was completed to Deakin of Bolton. In June 1919 a new Fowler B6 No. 14843 Reg. No. NC2021 named "Titan" was bought. The name plate and the works number for this engine came from the old "Titan" and so this engine ran as No. 10325. The old "Titan" was sold to P and H Shaw of Doncaster and No. 13036 the R3 Fowler called "Despatch" was also sold in March of 1919. Again in 1919 he bought two big McLarens from the War Office but later sold one, called "Goliath" to Pat Collins the showman. The second one was also later

11. — N.E. Box Manchester with Titan and Magic both with Boulton driving wheels at Oldham Boiler Works, May 1909.

12. — N.E. Box with Titan and Magic in position to winch the heavy girders up into position to carry the upper stories in a new hotel. Manchester, 1910.

sold, I'm not sure of its name, but it might have been "Bodicea". He also ran two German engines which he had received as reparations, driving crushers. These two were also eventually sold.

NORMAN E BOX — THE MAN

Norman E box was an extrovert or perhaps showman would be a better description. He never moved anything without having his photographers Messrs Entwistle Thorpe there to record the achievements for posterity. On long journeys he travelled with his engines often on foot, changing his socks and boots twice a day. On other occasions he would ride a push-bike as he escorted the load around the tight parts of the journey. His knowledge of Fowler engines was second to none and he realised that on the long journeys between Manchester and Birmingham to London or Liverpool, he could get a huge mileage out of the engines as Manchester to Liverpool was nearly all down hill. Thus the engine could haul nearly 100 tons to Liverpool while two engines would be required to pull the same load from Liverpool to Manchester.

He never had his engines delivering off a main road if he could possibly help it. He was the type of man who demanded forty miles from Manchester down the A34 and got it. As soon as an engine arrived new, off came the steerers seat in case the steerer fell asleep at the wheel. If he was standing he could jump off to put the trailer brakes on or shove a scotch in, without the seat being in his way.

If an engine driver became ill when Norman was travelling with the crew the he put him to bed in the van, and drove the engine himself. "Better two days in the van than a month in hospital," he used to say in such occasions. As the crew ran from pub to pub, a pint was put up to each man when they had completed their mileage target and had been signed for by the driver.

Being very astute he had the finest solicitor he could find who seldom if ever, lost a case. This was the controversial William Joynson - Hicks, nicknamed Jix.

JIX

William Joynson-Hicks, recently described in a Sunday Supplement as the Mary Whitehouse of his age, was born in 1865, the son of Henry Hicks a City Merchant. He became a solicitor in 1887, and married Grace Lynn Joynson, the daughter of a leading evangelist in 1895. The marriage explains his hyphenated name. In 1906 he stood for Parliament as a Conservative at North Manchester but was beaten by the then Liberal Churchill. When he later won the seat in the 1908 by-election, he received the nickname Jix.

He became M.P. for Brentford in 1911 and Twickenham in 1918. Although he was a spokesman at Westminster for Motor Transport, Aviation and Telephones, because he was at loggerheads with Lloyd George he did not at this time receive any office. In 1922 he defended General Dyer the perpetrator of the massacre of Amritsar in India. Also in 1922 he assisted with the overthrow of Lloyd George.

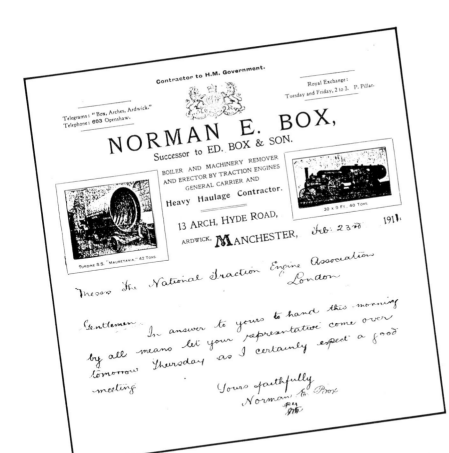

12a. — Letter heading of 1911.

13. — N.E. Box with Titan with heavy casting loaded on double Fowler built trailers 1912.

With Lloyd George removed Jix was free to seek political office. Between 1922 and 1924 he held various parliamentary offices before becoming Home Secretary in 1924, an office he held until 1929. He was thus Home Secretary during the General Strike of 1926. During his parliamentary career he helped to defeat the amended Prayer Book Act of 1928, he introduced the Shops Act of 1928, the so called shopworker's charter and introduced the 1928 Summer Time Act. He was preparing a Factories Act at the time of his party's defeat in the 1929 General Election.

A member of the Church Assembly and a strong evangelist he was created first Viscount Brentford in 1929, and died in 1932.

ENGINE TRAILERS AND EQUIPMENT

During 1922 the Manchester Water Department was laying water pipes from the dam in the Lake District to Manchester via Lancaster. Norman E. Box Ltd, won the contract to move these pipes and bought a new D5 Fowler No. 15785 Reg. No. NC6022, called "Ajax" to achieve this.

The McLaren "Magic" was sold around this time to Bates a showman of Rhode Heath. In June 1925 a new B6 Fowler No. 16263 Reg. No. NE2834 named "Talisman" was bought and in December of the next year another B6 joined the Box fleet. This was No. 16264 Reg. No. NF2032, named "JIX" after Norman's old friend, the solicitor. In 1928 "Vulcan" returned to Fowlers to have a crane fitted. The last new B6 with crane No. 17105 Reg. No. VM2110

named "Atlas" arrived in May of that year. Two second-hand Aveling and Porter compounds were purchased in 1929 from the Calico Printers Ass. This was an 8 NHP No. 6129 Reg. No. MA5317 and a 10 NHP No. 3570 Reg. No. MA9690.

Before 1924 Box owned two Fowler double bogie 8 wheeled flat trailers with solid tyres. One of these trailers was 24ft by 7ft 9ins, the other 18ft by 7ft 9ins, but both had a 3ft 10ins loading height with 70ton capacity each. These trailers had a steel plate across the middle drilled to take a swinging bolster. The short trailer had a slot to enable the centre to shorten and lengthen as the load negotiated the corners. Box also owned two Eagle double bogie 8 wheel flat trailers on solid tyres. Each trailer was 18ft by 7ft 9ins, with a 3ft 2ins loading height drilled for bolster work, with a 50 ton each capacity.

According to Fowler's records no heavy swan necked trailers were built for Box before 1928. The Fowlers did make a 10 ton swan neck in 1922. This trailer had an empty weight of 4T 15½ cwt. They also built a 15 ton swan neck on rubber solid tyres in 1923. Unfortunately the records do not state whether these trailers were a success or not. In October 1928 an 85 ton double swan necked trailer with two 8 wheel bogies was built. This trailer's rear wheels were fitted with screw brakes operating in brake drums. This monster had an empty weight of 31 tons. But even bigger trailers were built in October 1929 Dyson's built a 32 wheeled 110 ton capacity trailer (see transcript of telephone conversation with Mr Chaplin the designer).

14. — N.E. Box with Burrell 5 ton wagon No. 3494 and trailer case on wagon 3 tons, entablature on trailer 5 tons from Messrs Mirrlees Bickerton and Day for shipment 1913.

15. — N.E. Box with new R3 Fowler Despatch on left and McLaren Magic hauling 32 tons each to test two new ferro-concrete bridges over railways at Ashton under Lyne Lancs, 1913.

16. — N.E. Box from the rear the total weight of the two engines and loads being 96 tons, 1913.

17. — N.E. Box Despatch and Titan hauling a 60 ton rotor from Liverpool to Manchester Electricity Works 19/12/1913.

18. — N.E. Box Titan, Kitchener and Despatch complete with coal truck and living van leaving for Newcaste on Tyne with electrical machinery from Liverpool, 1914.

19. — N.E. Box Titan leading a hired 2 speed B6 Fowler No. 10142 assisting Despatch with second load of armoured steel plates for H.M.S. Malaya then building at Newcastle, 1914.

20. — N.E. Box at Trafford Park, Manchester with Titan wire-roping a 30 feet diameter x 24 feet deep chemical tank into position with Magic as anchor at Horrocks Chemical Works N.E.B. with raincoat. Usually moved on greasy plates, 1914.

Box also purchased between 1925 and 1929 three Scammells. One of these was a 25 tonner with gondola trailer to carry drums of electric cable. The second was another 25 tonner with a demountable axle Scammell 25 ton trailer, which had four double wheels in line on the rear. The last Scammell arrived in 1929 and it was a 45 tonner with its own Scammell trailer with demountable axle. All those vehicles had four speed gear boxes with changeable sprockets giving a larger range of speeds and power.

21. — N.E. Box with Kitchener tracing Titan hauling a large marine boiler about 75 tons carried on two Fowler bogies. Note wood packed wheels on Titan with coal truck and van, 1915.

22. — N.E. Box Titan without canopy hauling top section of a hydraulic press approx. 50 tons probably a short haul from railway to buyers premises, 1915.

23. — N.E. Box Despatch with a spherical mixer and ancilliary equipment, 1915.

THE BUTTERFLY COUPLING

This coupling was used to couple two steel wheeled bogies together. However the Box Butterfly coupling must not be confused with the Glasgow Butterfly Coupling which was used for an entirely different purpose. The Box system was for coupling two bogies together without using the drawbar or the Vee-bar. On the back of the front bogie a coupling box similar to the rear coupling on an engine was hinged on. This had three holes for pins. On the front of the rear bogie a hinged flat steel plate with a hole at each end and a slot running parallel to the width of the bogie. On a straight section a pin in each outside hole or one pin in the centre to allow for slight bends in the road. To make a sharp turn in the inside pin was removed allowing the outside pin to pull the bogie around. The two halves of the coupling were hinged so as to allow for changes in gradient, i.e. up over and down off a bridge.

ROADS AND LOADS

It would be impossible to recount every job ever carried out by the firm, even if we knew them all. Much of the work carried was for various electrical manufacturers. Messrs Siemens of Stafford, later to be known as English Electric Ltd, became a customer in 1912 and continued as such right up to the end. Metropolitan Vickers Ltd, of Manchester had Box moving large loads within the works, from one department to another. Although Box won this contract before 1914, it wasn't until 1922 that he hauled a load outside the works. Up until 1922 all big loads went out by rail on transporter wagons. Inside the works a railway Inspector and crew had an office from which he routed all loads to their various destinations. The whole works was covered by rail with the railway company dropping the wagons at the boundary and Metros own engines shunting them in. Later the L.M.S. took over the operation until they had a disagreement with Vickers and a gap was created which Norman Box walked into, taking over the contract. As the works was criss-crossed by rails it meant that every load had to be plated over the rails with round plates which were approximately three feet in diameter by ½ inch thick. These plates were scrap having been trepanned out of boiler ends for the fire boxes. They were purchased from Galloways and other boiler makers.

The laying of these plates was a dangerous process. The plates had to be placed under the preceeding one or else they kicked out with the chance, as had occasionally happened, that it might slice a leg off. If the transformer was being delivered to a power station or sub-station the heavy haulier usually had to place it on site. It was jacked up on the trailer with two flat bottom rails placed under it, one on each side. U-shaped channels would then be inverted on them with plenty of grease, then lowered to sit on the channels. This would then be packed up beneath the rails off the trailer and wire rope would be fixed to the engine's winch. The secret of this was to stop the winch at the right moment when the transformer was dead centre. Otherwise it would take about four hours to jack it back or forward an inch or two with the old Tangye water jacks. Strange to relate it is much harder to jack a large piece down rather than up, Great care has to be taken that it does not over balance if it is let down too fast or too quickly.

Moving Lancashire boilers was another mainstay of the firm, and of course they would not only be moved but also put into position. He quoted for many jobs in Wales but on examination one finds that the loads were delivered by Welsh sub-contractors. The loads were uplifted by Box photographed, and then hauled to an agreed spot near where the hill climbing began. This was not because the Box Fowlers were unable to climb hills, but because too much time would be wasted when the super lions could be more profitably employed running over the hard level roads on which they normally operated.

One subcontractor, the late E. T. Hughes of Llanrwst, delivered large quantities of machinery, excavators, boilers etc for Box. On one occasion Box's two Fowlers's arrived in the station yard at Llanrwst with a 30 foot by 9 foot Lancashire boiler in tow, to be delivered to CWM Machines Slate quarries. As usual prior arrangements had been made between Messrs Box and Hughes. It was understood that the boiler was correctly loaded, ready to be winched into position on arrival. Hughes took the word of an expert only to find when they arrived at the quarry, that the boiler was the wrong way round. There was no room to turn the trailer and after struggling up to the site they had to reverse all the way back to the station yard where the boiler had to be turned on the trailer. The engines used were an elderly Fowler convertible No. 3809 of 1879 and an old SCC Burrell of 1893, an 8 NHP. "That was the last time I took Mr Box's word on such a matter" said Mr Hughes emphatically.

Of course Norman and his men successfully erected into working position hundreds of boilers. One operation was in the centre of Manchester for Lewis the store group. One boiler was to be erected in place, then the store would be built around it. Arrangements had been made with Manchester Corporation Tramway to turn off the electricity for the wires after the morning rush hour. Unfortunately after the power had been switched off one tram stood stranded bang in the centre of where operations had to take place. Fred Dodd the foreman on the job called "Titan" which was running empty behind the load to tow the tram back clear of the area. "Titan" was to be used to wire rope the boiler into position.

One one occasion when Norman needed an engine for winching and discovered the only engine available was not licensed, he had it towed out then ran it up onto 3 inch planks. When the local policeman pulled him up about the license, Box told him that it was standing on his property not on the road. Sure enough when the policeman looked down the planks were branded N.E. Box Ltd.

24. — Said to be N.E. Box an interesting scene, no idea, 1915.

25. — N.E. Box Magic with armour plate from Cammell Laird & Co. Ltd. Sheffield for Birkenhead at Manchester docks where it was normally taken by lighter through the ship canal, 1915. N.E.B. on right of picture.

26. — N.E. Box Despatch hauling a 24 ton gun shield from Sheffield to Barrow in Furness, 1915.

27. — N.E. Box Garrett tractor No. 32680 of 1915 Bantam BJ 2486 with a hopper on what must have been the first swan necked trailer. Did it make the delivery before the trailor split in two, 1916.

On another occasion a Lancashire boiler had to go into a cotton mill in a conjested area of a local town. So conjested was the area that there was not enough room to turn an engine, let alone get a boiler in. Norman walked around the mill, and discovered that at the rear, the local canal ran past. He had all the holes in the boiler stopped up, and then launched in into the water. There with an engine on the opposite bank and a snatch block anchored at the rear of the mill, he pulled the boiler up onto the bank before running it into the boiler house.

At another mill the only road in for the boiler was down a hill. He was forced to bridge a canal then bounce the boiler over a wall which belonged to another party.

The secret of handling boilers is to get them as near upright when they come off the trailer. This might sound fairly straightforward, but it isn't as easy as one might think. If the boiler was lying dead centre, then three men with a winch might handle it with no major problems, but if it was off centre, then it would have to be turned by dancing it on two jacks. Since the men on the jacks might be perilously close to a wall, this was often an operation fraught with danger.

Tar macadam roads also proved a problem. When running on such roads in the height of summer the engine driving wheels would start to pick up the tar. An occasional pail of water thrown over the wheels helped but it was more convenient to work when the

day was cooler. Thus a normal working day would start before 5 a.m. and continue to about 11.30 a.m. The men would then have a break till 4 p.m. and run until 10 p.m. to make up the lost time. However this caused another problem. During the afternoon break the men had little to do except sit in a pub. This meant that going into a pub before noon and being thrown out at 3 p.m., half full of beer, the driver only had an hour to sober up sufficiently to drive the engine.

NORMAN AND THE LAW

By 1919 the legal weight for a road locomotive was 14 tons which allowed 50 cwts for the two driving wheels. This was made necessary for road adhesion as much as safety. The Bouldon system and Norman's own make of rear wheel were 3 tons each, being 6 tons for the pair. A traction engine so equipped proved itself equal to hauling loads of any weight, not only on the level but also up normal hills. Needless to say, for climbing really sharp hills, it was necessary to couple up a second engine. The additional weight of those wheels put the traction engine beyond the gross weight of 14 tons. It was not long before the police in various places were after him. So he devised the system of using a legal engine to haul the trailer on the flat and substituted an illegal one when a hill had to be tackled. The illegal engine would travel ahead of the load and as it was not pulling a large load would not attract the same attention. It was not Norman's business to flout the law, but he had to get around it or he would not have remained in business.

Around this time, the early twenties, county and borough surveyors in most parts of the country, but especially around Manchester, became increasingly concerned for the safety of their roads, as Norman moved loads of increasing weight. Concern led the surveyors to a course of action – the practice must be stopped. Accordingly Norman was invited to a London meeting of the County Surveyors Association. Presiding over this august body was Sir Henry Maybury, formerly of the Ministry of Transport. Also present was Mr (later Sir) John Thornycroft and Mr E.J. Strapnell-Smith. At this meeting, the Association made it clear to N.E. Box that he must limit the weight of his engines to 14 tons. Norman told the meeting as respectfully as he knew how, that they did not know what they were talking about. He pointed out the danger of using tractors which were too light and suggested that they make it their business to investigate for themselves. To help them in this he offered to demonstrate to any deputation that cared to come to Manchester just how useless a 14 ton locomotive was for hauling a heavy load over the Pennines. His offer was accepted and among those who came were the surveyors from Kent and Warwickshire. Seeing was believing! They saw that a 14 ton engine was incapable of handling a big load on such roads, whereas the heavier unit with the wooden block tyres put up a

faultless performance. It was not so very long before a new unit of 22 tons became the legal maximum. By 1922 Norman fitted his first engine with the new Mackintosh endless rubber tyres.

Readers should be aware that in the days of Norman E. Box some roads were very poor both in terms of surface and softness. Although they travelled most of England one part of the North-West which they kept away from, if at all possible, was Shap. The road from Shap into Scotland was unsuitable for heavy vehicles up to 1935 the only way into Scotland was up the A1 via Newcastle, that was why Scotland was never quoted.

ROUTE SURVEYS

By law every big load which was to be moved had to have its measurements exhaustively recorded. This was not simply a matter of recording its height when loaded but also such things on the route as overhead bridge heights, road bridge strengths and the width of roads, particularly at bends and corners. Thus a full survey of the proposed route had to be made. On one route it was noted that the street gas lamps were nearer the kerb than the prescribed 18 inches. Because these were going to interfere with the movement of a 28 foot wide load Norman wrote to the authority concerned. Politely, he informed this body that if they did not move the lamps, his vehicle would. Thus persuaded the authority acted.

28. — N.E. Box Garrett tractor Bantam with a better looking trailer, 1917.

29. — N.E. Box Titan with crane jib, moving machine in engineering works also without canopy, 1916.

30. — N.E. Box Magic hauling a 21 ton drying cylinder from Bolton to Manchester, 1916.

31. — N.E. Box Garrett Bantam with spectacular load a washing cylinder from Stevensons of Preston Lanc. 1916.
Note on canopy: OHMS WAR MATERIALS MUST NOT BE DELAYED EN ROUTE.

32. — N.E. Box Magic hauling 87 feet long girder for new gun shop at Armstrong Whitworths, 1916.

On another survey it was found that there would be only a fraction of an inch to spare when the load went under a railway bridge at Wetherby. In the event a train happened to pass over the bridge just as the load was underneath, the weight of the passing train was enough to suppress the bridge more than the spare fraction. The load got through but some of the bridge rivets were damaged.

More seriously, a passing load which was too heavy caused the partial collapse of another bridge. What was left of the bridge after the load was only enough for single lane traffic. A few days later an identical load was due to pass the same bridge. Norman considered the half width and decided to risk it. All went well but Norman was sued for damages for the collapsed half. However he successfully used the defense that it was the weakness of the collapsed half and not the weight of the load which was responsible.

Another bridge on the Warrington-Chester road was said to be so weak that passengers had to dismount before buses were allowed to cross. At the very moment that Mr Crosland-Taylor of Crosville Motor Services was giving evidence at an enquiry on the bridge a 30 ton tractor trailer outfit bearing the Norman E. Box Ltd. crossed it trouble free.

At no time did Norman Box ever lose a claim for road damages.

33. — N.E. Box Titan hauling three 10 ton crystallizers from Stockton on Tees to Northwich Cheshire with living van, 1918.

34. — N.E. Box Titan on right and Despatch hauling locomotive boilers and boxed parts from Nasmyth of Manchester for shipment. Approx. weight of each boiler 10 tons in M/C docks, 1918.

35. — N.E. Box Magic with three mooring buoys made by Nasmyth of Manchester, approx. 9 tons each, 1918.

36. — N.E. Box Titan with three mooring buoys made by Crossleys of Manchester to Stockton on Tees. On crossing the Pennines Titan would haul two trailers at a time over the steepest parts, 1918.

37. — N.E. Box Titan leading Vulcan hauling 45 ton marine boilers from Newcastle upon Tyne to Southampton with this height they would travel via Sunderland, Hetton Le Spring to Darlington then Thirsk, York, Tadcaster, Micklefield, Doncaster, Markham Moor, left via Lincoln road then right over level crossing to Stamford, Northampton, Towcester, Oxford and Winchester, 1919.

38. — N.E. Box Titan hauling 45 ton gear wheel on rigid bogie with no turning lock, to turn bogie uncouple one bar, July 1919.

39. — N.E. Box McLaren Rover with 22 ton steam crane on rigid bogie in Manchester, 1919.

40. — N.E. Box Vulcan with 30 ton, 70 feet launch from Oxford to Newcastle upon Tyne. With the position of the wooden wheeled truck at the rear it does not appear to have an engine in her, possible weight about 20 tons. The centre truck is a match truck without any weight being on it, 1919.

41. — N.E. Box Titan and Despatch coupled together for an unknown reason in Manchester, 1919.

42. — N.E. Box Titan leading Vulcan with marine boilers from Newcastle upon Tyne to Bristol weight approx. 30 tons each, 1919.

43. — N.E. Box Titan with storage tank approx. 15 tons, 1919.

44. — N.E. Box Titan rear view in Manchester, 1919.

45. — N.E. Box Titan with crane lifting a small tank, 1920.

46. — N.E. Box Garrett tractor 33713 Trojan with drums of cable. Note the super heater on smoke box, 1920.

47. — N.E. Box lowering a lancashire boiler down a slope as this was the only means of getting it into the boiler house, 1920.

48. — N.E. Box 30ft x 9ft boiler that after bridging the canal had to bounce it over a wall before gaining access to customers premises. Low arch prevented access by front door, 1920.

49. — N.E. Box another 30 footer being rolled over a temporary bridge by outside gang men. Note round plates to spread the weight when rollers pass over them. If an engine could not get near the job a Trewhella Monkey winch was used, this was a ratchet operated hand winch capable of pulling 50 tons direct or 70 tons with a snatch block, 1921.

50. — N.E. Box Vulcan winching a 70 ton anvil block onto the Great Western Railway Co. Ltd. Totem wagon normally used to carry large ingots. Specially sent up to the London North Western Railway Cos. yard for it. From B.S. Massey to Swindon. Note snatch block shackled to sling, 1922.

51. — N.E. Box Vulcan hauling two Cochran boilers. They would be unloaded using the winch. In Manchester, 1922.

52. — N.E. Box Vulcan with Condenser Casing from Bolton, 1922.

53. — N.E. Box Vulcan and Titan with Condenser 60 tons on rigid bogie. Built by Richardson Westgarth of West Hartlepool carried by sea to Manchester docks enroute to Barton Power Station note how near the top is to the tram wires, 1922.

54. — N.E. Box Vulcan and Titan with Condenser 60 tons loaded with heavy side to the centre of the road awaiting tramway overhead wire men to lift the wire under Patricroft Bridge, 1922.

55. – N.E. Box Vulcan with Lancashire boiler on two trailers, 1922.

56. — N.E. Box Vulcan and Titan at Manchester Corporation Electricity Works having hauled the 90 ton stator from Trafford Park. Loaded on rigid bogie with no turning lock, 1923.

57. — N.E. Box Titan hauling 20 ton transformers from Ferranti Manchester to Liverpool docks, 1924.

58. — N.E. Box Vulcan with Condenser 40 tons at Trafford Park, Manchester, 1924.

59. — N.E. Box Vulcan hauling a cast steel rudder hinge bracket enroute from Cammell Laird & Co. Ltd. Sheffield to Birkenhead for HMS Rodney. One of the many queer loads for a ships stern, approx. 30 tons, 1924.

60. — N.E. Box Vulcan after having first set of endless rubber tyres fitted to rear wheel. Note how small the snatch block hanging on rear coupling, 1924.

61. – N.E. Box Vulcan tracing Titan with transverter 40 tons from English Electric Co. Stafford to Wembley, 18/8/1924.

62. — N.E. Box Titan with 24 feet wide rudder casting for HMS Rodney at Birkenhead. Frame cast at Cammell Laird of Sheffield. Seen at Manchester docks, 1924.

63. — N.E. Box with cast steel propeller shaft bracket from Cammell Laird of Sheffield for HMS Rodney at Birkenhead approx. 35 tons, two required on twin screw ships, 1924.

64. — N.E. Box Titan otherside of load on No. 63, 1924.

65. — N.E. Box Vulcan tracing Titan with a 90 ton stator from Metro-Vickers Ltd. Trafford Park, Manchester to Manchester Corporation Electricity Works, 1924.

66. — N.E. Box Ajax parked in the Electricity Works waiting to take the empty bogie to the next job, 1924.

67. — N.E. Box Titan with steel casting on double bogie using butterfly and a platform on top for casting to sit on, 1924.

68. — N.E. Box Titan with two 12 to 15 ton low loading trailers loaded with cable drums, both trailers built by Fowler, 1924

69. — N.E. Box Titan front view of the two trailers, 1924.

70. — N.E. Box wire roping a 90 ton stator over round steel plates at Metro-Vickers works Manchester with Rover acting as anchor. Using a snatch block with wire returned to rear coupling, 1924.

71. — N.E. Box Stator in position to be lifted then Ajax Standing by to remove empty trailer in Manchester Corporation Electrical Works, 1924.

72. — N.E. Box Vulcan tracing Titan pulling partly dismantled excavator clear of low aquaduct. A No. 6 Ruston travelling on its own tracks, 1925.

73. — N.E. Box Galloway Lancashire boiler about to be lowered into basement of Lewis's new department store in Oxford Street, Manchester. Vulcan and Titan (behind boiler) one wire at each end. With Nelson Carpenter driver of Vulcan and Frank Morgan Manager of Manchester depot, 1925.

74. — N.E. Box Titan and Vulcan lowering the boiler down the timbers. Fred Dodd in trilby hat, 1925.

75. — N.E. Box The 30 ton 30 feet x 9 feet Lancashire boiler in place, 1925.

"CLEAN MA NAME!"

This was the order which all the following heard at one time or another. Sometimes it was in the yard, sometimes on customer's premises and sometimes when N.E.B.'s Bentley swept in front of them on the road.

Fred Dodd, general heavy lift foreman always stood with his thumbs thrust into his waistcoat arm holes. He knew all the answers, but never told a driver off in front of his crew, always took him out of hearing then let him have it.

George Wooler one of the early employees was "Titan" (I) driver, before becoming N.E.B.'s foreman fitter.

J. Harben was another early employee. He drove various engines, before becoming "Atlas" driver. He ended up as a foreman in Pickfords.

Nelson Carpenter started as driver on "Vulcan" in 1916 but was later promoted to foreman and transferred to the Lichfield depot in Birmingham when it opened in 1926. Nelson finished up as Pickford's general foreman.

Sid Calvert also started in 1916, first driving "Magic" and then "Rover" before becoming the last regular driver on "Atlas". Sid finished his working life as a mate on a Scammell.

A. Gifford, initially a Garrett tractor driver had a spell on "Magic", then went back to a tractor and eventually became a Scammell driver.

E. Mitchell had much the same career experience, being a Garrett tractor driver and then moving on to drive a 45 ton Scammell.

A. Calvert started as roller driver in Edinburgh, then moved onto "Ajax" when new work started on the Lancaster to Manchester water main. He took over "Jix" in 1928 in Birmingham where he finished as general foreman.

A. Parker initially a Garrett tractor driver, was the last regular driver of "Ajax" and finished as a foreman.

R. Bennett was the occasional driver of various engines. He had quite a spell on "Talisman" then under Pickfords became a Scammell driver.

R. Cruickshanks had an early history, noted for his demotion from "Vulcan" after he turned it over. Eventually he became driver of "Talisman" and left Pickfords after the war.

The history of N.E.B.'s steerers is as follows:— Walter Dearnley steered for J. Harben and finished as a mate; E. Simpson finished as a low loader mate; C. Simpson finished as General Foreman; J. Etchells finished in a gang; H. Smurthwaite finished as a Scammell driver; R. Flanagan's history is unknown; Fred Snelson (Blackjack) became a Bedford low loader driver; Frank Snelson became a foreman; W. Brooksbanks became a foreman; T. Mulston continued as steersman on the 32 wheeler; Fred Henshaw moved from Marsden Road Services to become a foreman. He became a Scammell driver, then led a gang and ended as general foreman in Pickfords.

This is not them all, the rest are lost in the mists of time. The office staff included:— Manager Frank Morgan at Maskell J. & M.K.; Cashier Will Ward promoted manager Box G. and S. Co. 1931; Inspector Les Harper promoted Manager at the Birmingham depot in 1926; Office Manager Tom Fishwick later Manager Box G. and S. Co.; Secrerary Miss Fishwick; Part-time Eunice Box.

76.— N.E. Box Ajax with a big wheel in Manchester, 1925.

77. — N.E. Box Talisman with a fly wheel and shaft used for generating electricity in a steel works. Note the bogie, this is the piano type with lower central axle. Bogie went flat at 60 tons normally, Manchester, 1926.

78. — N.E. Box Vulcan leading Talisman hauling 20 ton transformers from English Electric Co. Stafford. Note the living van with shelf underneath to carry lamps, slings etc. and rear shelf to carry sacks of coal, 1926.

79. — N.E. Box Talisman having hauled a 60 ton Condenser from Trafford Park to Manchester docks on a piano bogie, 1926.

80. — N.E. Box Ajax wire roping water pipes over a concrete bridge. Engine sitting on plates and timber, 1926.

81. — N.E. Box Vulcan and Titan wire roping through a snatch block fixed on top of the structure. Eight ton tanks into place at Anglo-American Oil Cos. refinery at Trafford Park, 1926.

82. — N.E. Box Vulcan and Titan although dated 1926 the author thinks it is 1923.

83. — N.E. Box the first of a new breed 25 tons Scammell with two small transformers going for shipment on gondola trailer approx. 18 tons, 1926.

84. — N.E. Box the engine shed with Titan, Jix, Talisman, Vulcan and Ajax at Rusholme Road, Ardwick, 1927.

85. — N.E. Box Titan with parts of 16 ins turrets for HMS Rodney at Manchester docks enroute to Birkenhead using a piano bogie and an eight wheel trailer plus a four wheel trailer weight about 20 tons each. Shipped to Birkenhead by lighter, 1927.

86. — N.E. Box Titan in Manchester Docks with gun turrets, 1927.

87. — N.E. Box Vulcan with other two sections of the gun turrets on four wheeled trailers, 1927.

88. — N.E. Box Vulcan and Titan behind awaiting arrival of lighter, 1927.

89. — N.E. Box Vulcan loading a 10 ton transformer on to a 25 ton Scammell, 1927.

90. — N.E. Box Titan hauling a 25 ton economy boiler, 1927.

91. — N.E. Box Titan after unloading boiler with winch, 1927.

A LIFE ON THE ROAD

Life on the road was hard and the men who worked on the road had to be harder. The 1933 Road Traffic Act improved conditions, but even after this date the brutal slog of road workers is difficult for us to understand. The Act ensured a maximum of eleven hours driving time a day and demanded that a log sheet be kept for all working hours. It also detailed minimum wages, known as the road haulage wages order, which included mimimun pay for all overtime worked. When this order came into force certain large firms dropped their wages when they realised that they had been over-paying their workers. It was certainly a fairer agreement than the practices which had been followed before. Not knowing what Norman's wages and conditions were we can only assume that they were fair or he would not have kept the good men.

In these days the men worked seven days a week, mostly every week, especially if they were away from home. In the winter they worked from early dark to late dark, as most loads could only be moved in daylight hours. They worked and moved their loads through ice and snow in freezing conditions. Holidays, were of course unpaid, they were paid to work and only to work seven days a week, away from home nearly all the time, one can only wonder how did they manage to get married and raise families.

Norman had a way with men and could always get the best out of them and make them want to give of their best. He had been known to bring Nelson Carpenter (who could easily have picked him up with one hand) down from a raging temper to a helpless laughing clown in a matter of seconds.

Then again he had a fair streak of temper in him. When hearing of an engine lying cold outside a certain pub at Birmingham, he picked up a driver and a steerer with the Bentley. The two reprobates were propped up against the pub wall, so full of rum that had their heads been tipped forward it would have run out of their mouths. They bundled the drunkards, into the back seat of the Bentley, before getting steam up and heading back with the engine to the yard. What was said to them nobody knows, but they were back on the job the next day.

Albert Calvert when driving "Ajax" the little Fowler was booked by the police for doing over 30 miles an hour in the city of Worcester. Now this was considerable speed in those days before 1930 when a IC wagon could only do about 24mph. Norman fought the case for him holding the policeman up for making a ridiculous statement as everyone knew that traction engines travelled at a top speed of only 12 mph. Albert did an empties run from Manchester to Rotherham and back in a day with "Ajax" at least once per month before being promoted to foreman. It was the fastest engine in the fleet at that time. The big B6's usually had a top speed of 27 mph but rarely did the drivers use the top speed even running solo because everything depended on the steerer and they only had the reverse lever to stop the engine.

Norman expected long hard hours out of his men, but they were his men and he gave of his best to them. No Box man need feel that if anything went wrong he was on his own. Norman backed them up all the way. When Bennett the spare driver was taken by

92. — N.E. Box Jix with another 25 ton boiler, 1927.

61

93. — N.E. Box Titan pushing boiler with a stick, 1927.

NEB in the Bentley to Liverpool to take over a B6 with empty trailer and run it back to Manchester, he was left by the roadside just outside the city. This was in case they missed the engine in Liverpool when it returned from the docks. Bennett always looked like a tramp and hanging about looked as if he was up to no good. A passing policeman looked him over and came to that conclusion just as NEB arrived following the engine. Fortunately the ubiquitous Entwhistle Thorpe photographer was in attendence. He had been doing another job and stopped to talk to NEB.

The Law should have moved on but he did not, instead he booked Bennett for acting suspiciously. Meanwhile the photographer was busy taking photos of the constable, including his number. NEB had Jix appear for Bennett. When the Magistrate saw the solicitor and then the photographs appearing for such a trivial offence the case was dropped.

However no-one could claim that Norman molly-coddled his men. Mr Sefton who married N.E.B.'s daughter became the manager after he had been taken to Edinburgh to see the northern operation. Driving back in the Bentley, Norman and Mr Sefton made up on one of his rollers travelling south down the A1. Flagging the driver into a wide part of the road N.E.B. told him to stop there for the night. When he bade him "Goodnight" the driver queried where he was to sleep since he had no living van. "In the coal truck" replied Norman. "But it's full of coal" responded the driver. "Aye it's best coal" said Norman "I've had to sleep amongst it many a time in the past,

so you should be alright". This was Seft's first encounter of Norman handling his staff after leaving the Air Force. Maybe he thought that he would have been better off in the R.A.F.

BOX GROUTING AND SPRAYING CO. LTD.

Broadheath:— The year was 1923 when N.E. Box purchased a yard at Broadheath and started to stock it with Fowlers Wood steamrollers. He also opened a depot in Edinburgh, calling the firm the "Box Grouting and Spraying Co. Ltd." it was widely rumoured that Fowler had shares in the company. However the author begs to differ. Fowler may have given him extended credit, but Fowler would need all his cash to keep his business going, because by then the steam business was falling off. If the reader studies the following vehicle purchasing list he will see that four rollers were lying in stock, three of them for two years and one for over a year. No! the author cannot see Fowler owning shares when the firm bought numerous Fodens even second-hand and ran Garrett tractors not Fowler tractors (SEE VEHICLE LIST page 94).

By 1940 they operated a Leyland petrol (feed) tanker to keep the sprayers working. This equipment worked up until 1948. In 1949 four new Foden diesel and one Leyland diesel tar-sprayers were purchased. At the end of 1946 several Marshall diesel rollers were bought off the Ministry of Supply. Two new Marshalls were acquired in 1950. Norman fell out with Marshalls over a faulty battery on one of the rollers and never dealt with them again. Most of his fleet of rollers were second-hand but he did buy the odd new Aveling-Barford.

The Foden steam wagons disappeared very quickly after 1948 but several Fowler rollers were kept. The last one was being used at Manchester Airport in 1958/59. This was kept in the yard afterwards until around 1961 when it was sold to Coles of Sleaford.

As well as the tar spraying side in the 1960's two Blaw Knox Asphalt layers were bought and hired out to County Council's and builders.

It is believed that the Edinburgh depot was closed after the war.

The Foden and Leyland diesels lasted well into the 60's. At least two of the Fodens were completely destroyed by separate fires in the early 60's. The diesel fired heating arrangement in the wrong hands proved devastating and with a tank full of 1000 gallons of Bitumen they were quickly burnt out.

Finally in the 1960's two Ford 6 wheel tar sprayers were purchased and these were used until the firm was wound up.

From the Altrincham depot contracts were carried out in Lancashire, Cheshire, Derbyshire, Yorkshire, Staffordshire and North Wales.

Norman operated various models of road traction engine but only one type of automobile. Even during the war he drove about in a 1930 Bentley and in

94. — N.E. Box Jix with 70 ton electric generator from English Electric Co. Stafford, to London Power Co., 1927.

95. — N.E. Box Jix tracing unkown with Lancashire boiler into a site, 1927.

96. — N.E. Box Talisman with Lancashire boiler at civic parade in Manchester after winning 1st prize in the class, 1927.

the 1950's a new one. At one time Norman had two Bentley's with the striking registration numbers of Box 1 and Box 2.

In 1959 "Box Grouting and Spraying Co. Ltd" became simple "Box and Co. Ltd."

THE GYROTILLER

In 1936 Fowler produced the gyrotiller. This was driven by a 180 hp M.A.N. diesel engine driving a machine consisting of two opposite rotating power driven rings of tillers. This machine could cut and crumble soil into small or large pieces as required, and to any depth up to 20 inches. This was a self-contained machine mounted on caterpillar tracks of an overall width less than the width filled. This meant that even the slight compression on the soil of the wide tracks is completely filled out by the rotating cutters.

The opportunities offered by this new machine were probably too good for Norman to let slip. Operating from Altrincham where one machine worked chiefly on the fields of Lord Derby's Knowsley Estate. In the Edinburgh depot the gyrotiller worked mainly in Fife. Norman's daughter opened a new depot at Peterborough to service East Anglia where two sometimes worked for Messrs Summers Ltd. of Lincoln the potato growers. Norman would call once a week, just to see how she was getting on. Unfortunately she was not doing so well. This was the only machine

operated by N.E.B. which was not a success. It tended to lift subsoil up to the surface when it was not set correctly. The small tractors then coming on the market effectively ousted the gyrotiller. Norman's machines operated as the Box Cultivating Co. Ltd. and N.E. Box Cultivators Ltd.

THE END

In January Norman approached J.N. Drummond head of Pickford's heavy haulage division, to see if they were willing to purchase the business. It was agreed that the sale would proceed for the sum of £80,000 plus Norman being retained at a handsome salary, for five years, as Manager. Thus on the 15th March, 1930 the firm of N.E. Box and Co. Ltd. passed into other hands. It was the end of an era.

Norman went over to Canada on holiday but took unwell while there. He ended up in hospital. Hearing what it was to cost he told the doctors "I am paying you plenty, so cure me". Unfortunately in health Norman did not get what he paid for and died in that Canadian hospital in 1957. Twenty-seven years after his company passed away, that genius of road steam haulage left this world.

EPILOGUE

So passed the life and the eventual death of an extraordinary man, a towering personality, who indelibly stamped his mark upon the history of British transport. But one question still remains. Why did he sell the heavy haulage side of his business in 1930? According to him it was because of the new legislation enacted in 1930. Could this really be true?

Norman E. Box was a man particularly attuned to the varied opportunities presented by heavy haulage. He moved into the trade in 1908, just as the steam road loco was coming into its own. Once in the business, he picked the right make for the job in hand, the B6. Box had after all operated a Fowler and a McLaren side by side in the early days and so could judge their relative merits. His preference for tractors was not in the direction of either Fowler or Burrells, but Garretts. Strangely, although Norman was a constant customer of Entwhistle Thorpe the photographers he didn't seem to care for publicity shots of the overworked Garretts. Indeed the only photos of these dependable servants come from private individuals.

Norman was not a man to fear experimentation and often tried out different models before deciding on the best tool for the job. Although he had two Garrett tractors converted into rollers by Messrs Fowler in 1923, he eventually decided that the Fowler-Wood was best suited to that work, and bought 17 of these machines over the years. Again he started out with Garretts on the haulage and spraying side of the business, then tried out a Sentinel steam wagon, but eventually came to prefer second-hand Fodens. As with the Garrett tractors, photos from this famous side of the business come exclusively from the public.

So he chose the Fowler road loco which suited the English terrain of hard fairly level roads, of course this was not the case in the Pennines and in Wales, but as we have seen he rarely entered Wales with his B6's. Also in the Pennines the roads, although steep in places had a hard surface which helped the drag considerably. Furthermore he found the use of block driving wheels were a great asset to his movements in this area.

Norman proved that his perception did not stop at being able to know a good engine, when he saw one. He once stated that his father could have papered his house with the summons he received from the police. Summons, were an occupational hazard and were equally attracted to Norman, hence his need for a really first class solicitor who could fight his court cases all over England. Of course he played tricks on local authorities. The town council at Macclesfield were determined to stop him from upsetting the traffic in the town centre. Norman was informed of this and on the next occasion a great noise was heard approaching the Town Hall. This turned out to be "Magic" hauling chains and pig-iron along the street while the load traversed a back road around the town centre.

97. — N.E. Box Vulcan wire roping a transformer onto site using old bogies as a bridge, 1927.

98. — N.E. Box Atlas hauling 43 ton of electrical material on the new 85 ton Fowler trailer from Metro Vickers to Trafford Park for export, 1928.

Having been brought up with traction engines he knew all the dodges. Double engine loads leaving Manchester for the South, would make Coven by night, leaving only a few hours for sleep, before the move through Wolverhampton after the last tram. Once clear of the overhead wires they would pull in on the Birmingham New Road, unless there was enough time to get through Brimingham too. Usually however they had to wait until after midnight before running through the city with their hurricane lamps. Normally they would stop for a few hours just off the tram track before coming onto daylight working again. The same process would be followed outside London, waiting until the last tram had gone before running into the city. This juggling with day and night moves married to superb man-management equalled efficiency.

In steam haulage Norman Box was a genius, so we must ask the question — did the man who so keenly understood this business foresee its end? Early in the 1920's a growing cloud rose to blot out the future of the steam traction engine. At this time the first articulated petrol engined Scammells began to appear. Based on the wartime Amercian Knox articulates, the first vehicles constructed were flat trailers, then as cable carriers. These were semi-low loading trailers, having a tail-gate which would be dropped to allow drums weighing approximately 2 tons to be loaded and unloaded, by hand winch on the swan neck. This was the principal vehicle which was to sound the death knell of the steam locos involvement in heavy haulage and consign these working engines to the scrap yard.

Before 1930, Scammells jumped from 15 tons, to a 25 ton model, to 45 tons then 100 tons came out. The 25 and 45 tonners had knockout near axles for end loading. A 100 ton vehicle was ordered by our old friends Marston Road Services, the same who bought over Edward Box and Co.

The 100 ton unit was delivered by Messrs Scammell and the trailer was a combined operation between E.C. Marston and Scammell. This remarkable vehicle was many years before its time. It was equipped with hydraulic rams to lift and lower the swan neck, originally by hand, and later by a single cylinder petrol engine. The trailer had two jockey wheels at the front which allowed it to be road taxed as a tractor and trailer at a third of the cost of an articulated, which of course, it was. The trailer was superimposed on top of the unit, and the vehicles motive power was a petrol engine developing 80 BPH. The same engine fitted all models over 10 tons.

Having an unladen weight of 30 tons the monster of the range was designed to accept a load of 100 tons, but during the last war it carried a load of 167 tons. With a forty foot wheelbase it was fitted with rear steering on the trailer. The manual steering on the front required seven complete turns of the wheel to go from lock to lock.

Delivered to Marston's in November 1929, this machine gulped about three gallons to the mile on a fairly level road, and about 5 gallons to the mile on heavy climbing. About three years later the chassis was lengthened and a Gardiner 6 LW diesel engine fitted which gave about 5 miles to the gallon, a remarkable saving. Another 100 tonner was built for a Cornish firm, but later found its way into the hands of Pickfords in Manchester.

If Norman did realise that these petrol engined machines could only mean the death of his beloved steam locos, his story about the 1930 law, is almost certainly deflection from the truth. The Act was at any rate fairly innocuous, principally insisting that 24 hours notice had to be given to each area which a load would pass through. Furthermore the law affected steam as well as petrol, and since Norman remained with Pickfords for another five years, he obviously did not foresee the end of haulage, only the participation of steam.

During that time A.E.C.'s, were added to the Pickfords fleet two of which had semi-low loading bodies built on an 8 wheeled chassis which travelled at 13 mph. All the Scammells had Gardner either 5 or 6 LW engines fitted in place of the original petrol models. Even the McLaren "Rover" had a Fowler

diesel fitted in place of the boiler and steam engine. This gave good pulling capacity but braking effectiveness was practically nil. The workers nicknamed it the "Haunted House" because of the frightening spectacle it made when bearing down on other road users.

The Scammells and the Amercan Diamond T which arrived as a tank transporter during the 1939 war finished the steam road loco forever.

Do you think that Norman saw it coming?

99. — N.E. Box Talisman hauling 60 ton piece of electrical equipment from Metro Vickers of Trafford Park for export, 1928.

100. — N.E. Box Jix tracing Atlas, hauling an 80 ton turbo alternator from GEC Ltd. works, Witton, Birmingham enroute to Liverpool for shipment to Adelaide, Australia, 1929.

101. — N.E. Box Vulcan tracing Atlas with a transformer 70 tons from Metro Vickers of Trafford Park on Fowler eight wheeled flat trailer, 1929.

102. — N.E. Box Talisman tracing Atlas with 90 ton stator, 1929.

103. — Who left the road in this mess, was it N.E.B.?, 1929.

104. — N.E. Box Titan wire roping a stone. Note timbers to protect wire at corners, 1929.

105. — N.E. Box stone along side bogie before winching on, 1929.

106. — N.E. Box bogie complete with stone now on road ready for Titan to deliver to Manchester University for students of sculpture to practice on, 1929.

107. — N.E. Box Titan barking up the bank, 1929.

108. — N.E. Box Vulcan between Rivington and Anglezark near Chorley with a boiler, 1929.

109. — N.E. Box Vulcan on arrival at Dolgarrog, North Wales to erect a turbine. Sundries on Eagle trailer, 1929.

110. — N.E. Box Vulcan unloading Eagle trailer, 1929.

111. — N.E. Box with 30 ft x 8'-6" Lancashire boiler 28 tons travelling over a makeshift bridge old trailer on rollers at Bradford Mill, 1929.

112. — N.E. Box making headway, 1929.

113. — N.E. Box 85 ton generator on Fowler trailer with a slight bend at both swan necks, 1929.

114. — N.E. Box Talisman with rudder and pintle approx. 35 tons on 40 ton Eagle trailer loaded at Harland & Wolff, Liverpool. Canted on trailer to allow other traffic to pass, 1930.

115. — N.E. Box as 114 from other side, 1930.

116. — N.E. Box as 114 view from rear, 1930.

117. — N.E. Box Atlas with R.A.F. launch on two Eagle trailers built at Harland & Wolff Ltd., Liverpool, 1930.

118. — N.E. Box Talisman and Atlas with transformer on Fowler flat trailers about 50 tons each, 1930.

119. — N.E. Box Atlas with a 105 ton Ferranti transformer on the 32 wheeler Dyson trailer that was built by Cranes of Dereham this is the finest trailer produced for heavy haulage at that time taken at Barton Power Station, 1930.

120. — N.E. Box Talisman and Atlas with 137 ton on the 32 wheeler trailer, 1930.

100 ton — 32 wheel trailer — pictured here was built in 1928 for Dyson by the company of Messrs Crane Ltd., Dareham, Norfolk. The designer was Mr W. D. Chaplin who dictated the following information over the telephone:—

We received an enquiry on a small printed card having a half-penny stamp for 100 ton trailer. We were then working in with R.A. Dyson and Co. and we queried if it should have read 10 ton trailer but we heard it was for loading 110 tons.

I was 24 years of age then and was a one man drawing office and was interested in the design of the vehicle. Soon certain preliminary outline drawings were presented for N.E. Box consideration. It was approved and design details were then proceeded with. Actually I personally made every drawing of the necessary components, having a flair for original thinking and the massive steel cast were made in the work Union Des Acieries at Cherletoi, Belgium from which the load carrying platform was made to my drawings by Danks of Netherton. The rather complicated bogey frame was made in the works at Dereham under the foremanship of Mr E.G. Harbour.

The vehicle was completed and approved and appeared on Dyson's stand at Olympia September/October 1929.

Incidentally a much larger load of 167 tons was carried some years later on the trailer.

Certain details are as follows:—
8 axles 4 wheels each with 2 26" diameter tyres making 64 tyres in all.

Brakes were first on inner wheels only but later fitted on outer.

Internal expanding brake shoes operated by lockhead wheel cylinder. All wheels on S.K.F. ball-bearings one being 10" diameter and having 1¼" diameter balls (or maybe 30mm).

All wheels steered without scuffing with tyres on true ACKERMANN principle. Each bogey was designed to carry load when required.

The weight of the total unit was 32 tons.

Dictated by Mr W.D. Chaplin over the telephone

121. — N.E. Box Atlas with 80 ton on front half of the 32 wheeler a transformer from British Thomson Houson Co., Rugby, 1930.

122. – N.E. Box 45 ton Scammell with Ruston steam navvy approx. 45 ton. Note Trewhella Monkey winch lying on bend of swan neck holding navvy forward, 1930.

123. — N.E. Box four Scammells each carrying condenser shells 14 feet wide from Metro Vickers Trafford Park to Portishead Electric Works, 1930.

124. — Explains it all, 1930.

NORMAN E. BOX LIMITED

MANCHESTER AND BIRMINGHAM

DINNER

Held at the Engineers' Club, Manchester
SATURDAY, MARCH 15th, 1930
to inaugurate the Amalgamation
of the firm with Messrs.
Pickfords Ltd.

❖

Chairman: NORMAN E. BOX

125. — Box Grouting and Spraying Co. Ltd.
12 ton roller Fowler-Wood roller, 1923.

126. — Box Grouting and Spraying Co. Ltd. Foden 6 ton LG 6258 of 1931.

127. — Box Grouting and Spraying Co. Ltd. Altricham Foden sprayer LG 8805, 1932.

128. — Box Grouting and Spraying Co. Ltd. Altrincham Foden sprayer MB 7860, 1936.

129. — N.E. Box Sentinel AW 6695 worked with the Grouting & Spraying Co., 1931.

130. — Box Grouting and Spraying Co. Ltd. Sentinel, LC 6919, 1931.

131. — N.E. Box the great man himself, 1950.

132. — Pickfords after the take over 120 tons transformer on 32 wheeler closed up. The reader can see how easy it would be to be caught by the wheels when turning the brake or steering wheels, three brakes men killed by this trailer.

133. — Pickfords Accumulator from Annan to Rotherham. Note the extended 32 wheeler, the geometry of the steering on the rear section is such that it follows the front half without any hang in at corners. Some bandit defaced the only negative in existence of this movement. Bogies 60 ft. apart. Jix tracing Atlas with Talisman following 90 tons, 1938.

134. — MRS Ltd. 45 ton Scammell with 36 ton stern frame 18 feet x 4 ins. wide from Sheffield to Glasgow, 1936.

135. — MRS Ltd. Bridge section being moved by two Fowlers KD 2826 and ME 7115, 1934.

136. — MRS Ltd. 45 ton Scammell with one of the propellors for the "Queen Mary", 1934.

137. — Marstons Road Services Ltd. Fowler KD 2826 with alternator on Eagle trailer, 1929.

138. — MRS Ltd. with original cab KD 9168 the World's largest lorry. Carrying capacity 100 tons, 1931.

139. — Edward Box Ltd. with new cab KD 9168 with diesel engine fitted replacing petrol 4 cyl engine heaviest load moved 167 tons, 1947.

140. — Edward Box Ltd. KD 2826 ex. Sheffield with 109 ton loaded between and 80 ton home built 4 axle trailer and a home built monkey mounted on Sentinel DG 6 double bogies traced by a Scammell Pioneer tractor enroute to Liverpool for Russia, 1939.

141. — Edward Box Ltd. KD 2826 traced by Scammell Pioneer Tractor hauling 66 ton tower, 1939.

142. — Edward Box Ltd. 100 ton Scammell unit hauling the tower into the dock, 1939.

143. — Edward Box Ltd. 45 ton Scammell with local Birmingham job. Note box on radiator, 1947.

144. — N.E. Box Titan B6 Fowler No. 10325 new Oct. 1906.

145. — N.E. Box Titan B6 Fowler No. 14843 new June 1919.

146. — N.E. Box Magic 8 NHP McLaren No. 1053 new May 1909.

147. — N.E. Box Rover 8 NHP McLaren No. 1570 new March 1918.

148. — N.E. Box Vulcan B6 Fowler No. 14844 new Oct. 1916.

149. — N.E. Box Ajax D5 Fowler No. 15785 new Jan. 1922.

150. — N.E. Box Atlas B6 Fowler No. 17105 new May 1928.

151. — Box Grouting and Spraying Co. Ltd. advertisement.

BOX GROUTING & SPRAYING CO. LTD. — STEAM LIST OF ROLLERS, WAGONS AND ENGINES

	BOUGHT FROM	REG. No.	MAKER & No.	YEAR	TYPE	SOLD TO
1	1923 New	NC 3986	J. Fowler 15814	7/21	10 Ton Roller	Douglas Corporation
2	1923 New	NC 5103	J. Fowler 14677	10/21	12 Ton Roller	Liverpool Corporation
3	1923 New	NC 5104	J. Fowler 14678	10/21	12 Ton Roller	Sold 9/50
4	1923 New	NW 1456	J. Fowler 15705	5/22	10 Ton Roller	Sold 9/50
5	1923 New	NW 2886	J. Fowler 15996	1/23	12 Ton Roller	Sold 12/51
6	1923 New	NW 3276	J. Fowler 16004	3/23	10 Ton Roller	D. Wood Yeadon 6/39
7	1923 New	NW 4058	J. Fowler 16007	5/23	10 Ton Roller	IOM Highways 8/25
8	1924 New	NW 6276	J. Fowler 16196	3/24	12 Ton Roller	S. Hutton & Co. 9/50
9	1924 New	NW 6771	J. Fowler 16241	4/24	10 Ton Roller	D. Wood & Co. 9/54
10	1925 New	UM 524	J. Fowler 16435	4/25	12 Ton Roller	11/50
11	1926 New	UM 3919	J. Fowler 16664	3/26	12 Ton Roller	Northn. G & G Arbroath /39
12	1926 New	UM 3918	J. Fowler 16665	4/26	12 Ton Roller	AM Cole, Gleaford /57
13	1926 New	UM 4177	J. Fowler 16666	4/26	12 Ton Roller	-
14	1927 New	UM 9089	J. Fowler 16970	4/27	12 Ton Roller	Kings & Co. Glw. /51
15	1927 New	UA 1446	J. Fowler 17503	11/27	12 Ton Roller	/51
16	1928 New	UA 3749	J. Fowler 17882	4/28	12 Ton Roller	/50
17	1929 New	UB 315	J. Fowler 18429	5/29	12 Ton Roller	Kings & Co. 1/42
18	1923 ex Bowland RDC	WY 6727	J. Fowler 9029	5/01	12 Ton Roller	Newton in Makerfield /26
19	1931 ex Bomford & Evershead	TB 2720	Aveling & Porter 6345	8/07	8 Ton Roller	Sold /33
20	1928 ex Millar Blackburn	CB 3053	Aveling & Porter 2557	10/89	12½ Ton Roller	Duncan Laurancekirk /30
21	4/40 Estate	GTU 162	McLaren 572	6/96	8 NHP Traction Engine	Love Stretford 10/40
22	12/30 Barron St. Helens	TE 1503	Foden 12718	8/27	6 Ton Wagon	
23	/33 Harrison Stretford	M8 284	Foden 6120	13/16	5 Ton Wagon	
24	/33 Harrison Stretford	TC 2336	Foden 10732	2/23	5 Ton Wagon	Scrapped 33 or 34
25	12/30 Ac Clark, Wigan	TE 309	Foden 11522	/23	6 Ton Wagon	Sold /36
26	7/34 I & A Jackson, Longsight	NE 5478	Foden 17074	2/26	6 Ton Wagon	Sold /33
27	/37 F.T. Wood	WX 4998	Foden 13700	7/30	6 Ton Wagon	
28	/37 Seakin Whitchurch	UX 5258	Foden 13210	/28	6 Ton Wagon	
29	/37 Riding & Gillow Bacup	TF 3106	Foden 13764	9/30	6 Ton Wagon	
30	/37 Riding & Gillow Bacup	LG 6258	Foden 13804	2/31	6 Ton Wagon	Mechanical TS & G Co. Reading 9/50
31	/31 WT & A Jackson	TE 8437	Foden 13404	6/29	6 Ton Waggon	/46
32	/31 New	LG 6919	Super Sentinel 8547	5/31	6 Ton Waggon	/46
33	/32 New	LG 8805	Foden 14074	2/32	6 Ton Wagon	D. Wood & Co. /44
34	/32 New	LG 8887	Foden 14072	2/32	6 Ton Wagon	D. Wood & Co. /44
35	/33 HV Smith & Co.	MB 7860	Foden 11702	3/25	6 Ton Wagon	9/50
36	Hancock	MP 1724	Foden 12740	1/28	6 Ton Wagon	9/50
37	Parkers of Burslem	EH 5904	Foden 11590	12/24	6 Ton Waggon	11/46
38		AW 6695	Super Sentinel 2987		6 Ton Waggon	
39	Angus CC	SR 1484	Tasker 1767	12/18	5 Ton Tractor	

In addition the Box Grouting & Spraying Co. Ltd. owned four Garrett Tractors which were changed by Fowler to Rollers.

GOING ON TO THE LAND

FRONT VIEW. NOTE COMPACT CONSTRUCTION

THE GYROTILLER

STANDING

What it is.

A machine consisting of two oppositely rotating power driven rings of tillers, which cut and crumble the soil in small or large pieces as required, and to any depth desired up to 20".

A self-contained machine mounted on Caterpillar tracks of an overall width considerably less than the width tilled, so that even the slight compression on the soil by the wide tracks is completely tilled out by the rotating cutters.

Has been built with an ample reserve of power so that no soil should prove too hard or too heavy for it.

On arrival at a field takes about five minutes to lower the tillers and commence work.

APPENDIX

MARSTON'S ROAD SERVICES IN ASSOCIATION WITH EDWARD BOX

This business was never part of the previously mentioned firms. Marston bought over the original E. Box business when Edward died in 1925. The author does not know the conditions of sale but when the name appeared on Scammells and Fowlers, Messrs Pickfords served a writ on them (presumably because after buying Norman's business they owned the name N.E. Box and Co. Ltd.) After a long battle in court Pickfords lost the case.

M.R.S. had been reconstituted after a fire at Edward Box Ltd. under Colonel Hudson of the owners Hauliers Ltd. The name appeared on Fowler KD 2826 No. 17106 a B6 with crane and ex NEB's Fowler VA 2464 No. 17293. DN. class tractor 5 NPH and the world's largest lorry the 100 ton Scammell KD 9168. The 100 tonner was still carrying this name after nationalisation when it arrived in Glasgow to haul railway locomotives to the docks.

THE END